Books by Virginia A. Tashjian

ONCE THERE WAS AND WAS NOT
Illustrated by Nonny Hogrogian

JUBA THIS AND JUBA THAT
Illustrated by Victoria de Larrea

THREE APPLES FELL FROM HEAVEN
Illustrated by Nonny Hogrogian

WITH A DEEP SEA SMILE
Illustrated by Rosemary Wells

WITH A DEEP SEA SMILE

WITH A DEEP SEA SMILE

STORY HOUR STRETCHES
FOR LARGE OR SMALL GROUPS

Selected by
Virginia A. Tashjian

Illustrated by
Rosemary Wells

Little, Brown and Company

BOSTON · TORONTO

TEXT COPYRIGHT © 1974 BY VIRGINIA A. TASHJIAN

ILLUSTRATIONS COPYRIGHT © 1974 BY ROSEMARY WELLS

Third Printing

T03/74

Acknowledgments for permission to reprint material in this book may
be found on page 130.

Library of Congress Cataloging in Publication Data

Tashjian, Virginia A   comp.
   With a deep sea smile.

   SUMMARY: A collection of chants, poems, stories,
finger plays, riddles, songs, and jokes which may be
used by a leader with a group.
   [1. Children's literature (Collections)
[1. Literature--Collections. 2. Storytelling--
Collections] I. Wells, Rosemary, illus. II. Title.
PZ5.T287Wi   808.8   72-8874
ISBN 0-316-83216-2

Published simultaneously in Canada
by Little, Brown & Company (Canada) Limited

PRINTED IN THE UNITED STATES OF AMERICA

For My Three Boys:
Kenneth Shant
Roy Shahan
Douglas Sevan
from Dud

CONTENTS

xi

TO BOYS AND GIRLS

IF you enjoy sharing stories, poems, chants, finger plays, riddles, songs, tongue twisters and jokes with your friends and neighbors, you will want to try the ones in this book.

These have been popular with children in library story hours; indeed, some of them have been made up by story hour listeners right in the library. Perhaps you can make up some of your own.

WITH A DEEP SEA SMILE

CHANTS

Chants are usually accompanied by hand slapping, changing rhythms and voice pitch, clapping of hands and shaking of the head. Follow the leader in these well-known chants and have fun.

A FOR APPLE

Starting with A, the leader goes through the alphabet, giving each letter and then adding a word which begins with that letter. He continues until he or the group fails to keep up. Then a new leader is chosen.

Leader:	Oh, I say A.	
Response:	Oh, I say A.	
Leader:	A for apple.	
Response:	A for apple.	
Leader:	And I say B.	A for apple and B for boy.
Response:	And I say B.	A for apple and B for boy.
Leader:	And I say C. for Carol.	A for apple and B for boy and C for Carol.
Response:	And I say C. for Carol.	A for apple and B for boy and C for Carol.

THE GREEN GRASS GROWING ALL AROUND

Many people know this as a song; it is equally effective as a chant. Keep a sing-song cadence as you chant faster and faster.

There was a tree stood in the ground,
The prettiest tree you ever did see;
The tree in the wood, and the wood in the ground,
And the green grass growing all around,
And the green grass growing all around.

And on this tree there was a limb,
The prettiest limb you ever did see;
The limb on the tree, and the tree in the wood,
The tree in the wood, and wood in the ground,
And the green grass growing all around,
And the green grass growing all around.

And on this limb there was a bough,
The prettiest bough you ever did see;
The bough on the limb, and the limb on the tree,
The limb on the tree, and the tree in the wood,
The tree in the wood, and the wood in the ground,
And the green grass growing all around,
And the green grass growing all around.

Now on this bough there was a nest,
The prettiest nest you ever did see;
The nest on the bough, and the bough on the limb,
The bough on the limb, and the limb on the tree,
The limb on the tree, and the tree in the wood,
The tree in the wood, and the wood in the ground,
And the green grass growing all around,
And the green grass growing all around.

And in the nest there were some eggs,
The prettiest eggs you ever did see;
Eggs in the nest, and the nest on the bough,
The nest on the bough, and the bough on the limb,
The bough on the limb, and the limb on the tree,
The limb on the tree, and the tree in the wood,
The tree in the wood, and the wood in the ground,
And the green grass growing all around,
And the green grass growing all around.

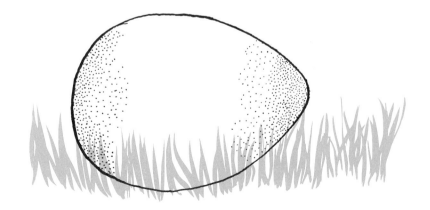

THE OLD WOMAN AND THE PIG

Everyone claps on the response only. This old song is equally effective as a chant. A slight pause after the third "oink" makes a better rhythm.

Leader: There was an old woman, and she had a little pig.

Audience: Oink, oink, oink—oink, oink, oink.

Leader: There was an old woman and she had a little pig,
He didn't cost much 'cause he wasn't very big.

Audience: Oink, oink, oink—oink, oink, oink.

Leader: This little old woman kept the pig in the barn.

Audience: Oink, oink, oink—oink, oink, oink.

Leader: This little woman kept the pig in the barn,
The prettiest thing she had on the farm.
Audience: Oink, oink, oink—oink, oink, oink.
Leader: But that little pig did a heap of harm,
Audience: Oink, oink, oink—oink, oink, oink.
Leader: But that little pig did a heap of harm,
He made little tracks all around the barn.
Audience: Oink, oink, oink—oink, oink, oink.
Leader: The little old woman fed the pig on clover.
Audience: Oink, oink, oink—oink, oink, oink.
Leader: The little old woman fed the pig on clover,
And when he died, he died all over.
Audience: Oink, oink, oink—oink, oink, oink.

MERRY MACK

Repeat the words slowly at first—and then faster and faster and faster! Accompany the words with a four-motion "pease porridge" type of clapping in rhythm: touch lap with both hands open flat, clap hands, touch outstretched hands of neighbor, clap hands. Keep repeating in rhythm.

Oh Merry Mack, Mack, Mack,
All dressed in black, black, black.

With silver buttons, buttons, buttons,
All down her back, back, back.

She cannot read, read, read,
She cannot write, write, write.

But she can smoke, smoke, smoke,
Her father's pipe, pipe, pipe.

She asked her mother, mother, mother,
For fifty cents, cents, cents.

To see the elephant, elephant, elephant,
Jump the fence, fence, fence.

He jumped so high, high, high,
He reached the sky, sky, sky.

And he never came back, back, back,
Till the fourth of July, July, July.

THIS IS THE KEY

The leader reads through both verses slowly. Then he reads the first verse slowly in rhythmic cadence. The group responds with the second verse, reciting the lines faster and faster!

This is the Key of the Kingdom:
In that Kingdom there is a city;
In that city there is a town;
In that town there is a street;
In that street there winds a lane;
In that lane there is a yard;
In that yard there is a house;
In that house there waits a room;
In that room an empty bed;
And on that bed a basket—
A Basket of Sweet Flowers:
    Of Flowers, of Flowers;
    A Basket of Sweet Flowers.

Flowers in a basket;
Basket on the bed;
Bed in the chamber;

Chamber in the house;
House in the weedy yard;
Yard in the winding lane;
Lane in the broad street;
Street in the high town;
Town in the city;
City in the Kingdom—
This is the Key of the Kingdom;
Of the Kingdom this is the Key.

HEAD AND SHOULDERS, KNEES AND TOES

The leader goes through the motions once slowly—and then, all join in. The first time, do the actions slowly; go faster and faster until the fourth time, when all actions are being performed at top speed.

Head and shoulders, knees and toes,
Knees and toes, knees and toes!
Head and shoulders, knees and toes,
Clap your hands and around you go!

MOMMA, MOMMA, HAVE YOU HEARD?

This can be sung, but it is very effective as a chant accompanied by clapping of hands and stamping of feet in rhythm. The leader should chant in accented cadence; the audience will soon join in.

Momma, Momma, have you heard?
Poppa's gonna buy me a mocking bird,

If that mocking bird don't sing,
Poppa's gonna buy me a diamond ring,

If that diamond ring don't shine,
Poppa's gonna buy me a bottle of wine,

If that bottle of wine gets broke,
Poppa's gonna buy me a billy-goat,

If that bill-goat runs away,
Poppa's gonna spank my boomsy-ay,

If my boomsy-ay gets sore,
Poppa's gonna buy me a grocery store,

If that grocery store burns down,
Poppa's gonna buy me an evening gown,

If that evening gown don't fit,
Poppa's gonna say "I quit, quit, quit!"

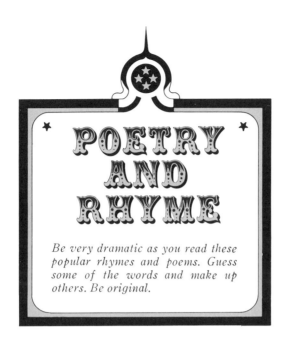

POETRY AND RHYME

Be very dramatic as you read these popular rhymes and poems. Guess some of the words and make up others. Be original.

THE STORY OF AUGUSTUS
WHO WOULD NOT HAVE ANY SOUP

The audience joins in the refrain.

Augustus was a chubby lad;
Fat ruddy cheeks Augustus had;
And everybody saw with joy,
The plump and hearty healthy boy.
He ate and drank as he was told,
And never let his soup get cold.
But one day, one cold winter's day,
He screamed out — "Take the soup away!
Oh take the nasty soup away!
I won't have any soup today!"

How lank and lean Augustus grows!
Next day he scarcely fills his clothes,
Yet, though he feels so weak and ill,
The naughty fellow cries out still—
"Not any soup for me, I say:
Oh take the nasty soup away!
I won't have any soup today!"

The third day comes; ah! what a sin!
To make himself so pale and thin.
Yet, when the soup is put on table,

He screams as loud as he is able —
"Not any soup for me, I say:
Oh take that nasty soup away!
I won't have any soup today!"

Look at him, now the fourth day's come!
He scarcely weighs a sugar-plum;
He's like a little bit of thread,
And on the fifth day he was — DEAD!

                —Heinrich Hoffman

LIMERICKS

There was an old man of Blackheath,
Who sat on his set of false teeth.
    Said he, with a start,
    "O Lord, bless my heart!
I've bitten myself underneath!"

        A silly fellow named Hyde
        In a funeral procession was spied.
            When asked, "Who is dead?"
            He giggled and said,
        "I don't know; I just came for the ride."

There was an old fellow who when little
Fell casually into a kettle.
    But, growing too stout,
    He could never get out,
So he passed all his life in that kettle.

        A cheerful old bear at the zoo
        Could always find something to do.
            When it bored him, you know,
            To walk to and fro,
        He reversed it and walked fro and to.

There was a young man from the city
Who met what he thought was a kitty.
     He gave it a pat
     And said, "Nice little cat."
And they buried his clothes out of pity.

There was a young lady from Crete
Who was exceedingly neat.
     When she got out of bed
     She stood on her head
To keep from soiling her feet.

There was an old person of Dean
Who dined on one pea and one bean.
     For he said, "More than that,
     Would make me too fat,"
That cautious old person of Dean.

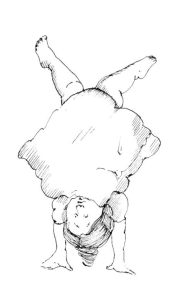

JEREMIAH

The leader should hesitate on the last word of every other line and let the listeners supply the rhyme.

Jeremiah
Jumped in the fire.
Fire was so hot
He jumped in the ——— (pot).
Pot was so little
He jumped in the ——— (kettle).
Kettle was so black
He jumped in the ——— (crack).
Crack was so high
He jumped in the ——— (sky).
Sky was so blue
He jumped in a ——— (canoe).
Canoe was so deep
He jumped in the ——— (creek).
Creek was so shallow
He jumped in the ——— (tallow).
Tallow was so soft
He jumped in the ——— (loft).
Loft was so rotten
He jumped in the ——— (cotton).
Cotton was so white
He jumped all ——— (night).

THE FISH WITH
THE DEEP SEA SMILE

The leader should recite this alone once. The listeners will chime in the second time—especially on the refrain.

They fished and they fished
Way down in the sea,
Down in the sea a mile.
They fished among all the fish in the sea,
For the fish with the deep sea smile.

One fish came up from the deep of the sea,
From down in the sea a mile,
It had blue-green eyes
And whiskers three
But never a deep sea smile.

One fish came from the deep of the sea,
From down in the sea a mile.
With electric lights up and down his tail,
But never a deep sea smile.

They fished and they fished
Way down in the sea,
Down in the sea a mile.
They fished among all the fish in the sea,
For the fish with a deep sea smile.

One fish came up with terrible teeth,
One fish with long strong jaws,
One fish came up with long stalked eyes,
One fish with terrible claws.

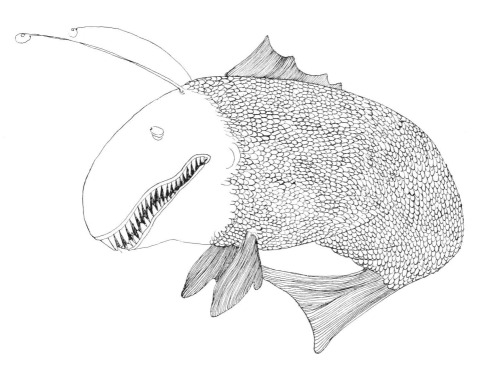

They fished all through the ocean deep,
For many and many a mile.
And they caught a fish with a laughing eye,
But none with a deep sea smile.

And then one day they got a pull,
From down in the sea a mile.
And when they pulled the fish into the boat,
HE SMILED A DEEP SEA SMILE.

And as he smiled, the hook got free,
And then, what a deep sea smile!
He flipped his tail and swam away,
Down in the sea a mile.

—*Margaret Wise Brown*

SENSE-LESS RHYMES

Mary had a little lamb,
Its fleece was white as snow!
And everywhere that Mary went
—She took the bus.

Hickory Dickory Dock,
The mouse ran up the clock;
The clock struck one
—Time for lunch!

Georgie Porgie, pudding and pie
Kissed the girls and made them cry;
When the boys came out to play
—The girls were mad!

Hot-cross buns!
Hot-cross buns!
One a penny, two a penny,
—Pretty cheap!

The last two sense-less rhymes were made up by children in a library story hour. Can you make up some, too?

BOYS' NAMES

What splendid names for boys there are!
There's Carol like a rolling car,
And Martin like a flying bird,
And Adam like the Lord's First Word,
And Raymond like the harvest Moon,
And Peter like a piper's tune,
And Alan like the flowing on
Of water. And there's John, like John.

GIRLS' NAMES

What lovely names for girls there are!
There's Stella like the Evening Star,
And Sylvia like a rustling tree,
And Lola like a melody,
And Flora like a flowery morn,
And Sheila like a field of corn,
And Melusina like the moan
Of water. And there's Joan, like Joan.

—Eleanor Farjeon

Ask for other names in the group and make up rhymes to fit. Here are some examples made up by children in a library story hour.

There's Douglas like a black fir tree,
And Dicky like a bird that's free.

There's Louise like a China vase,
And Mary like silvery lace.

There's Ralph like a spinning top,
And Tommy like some soda pop.

OVER IN THE MEADOW

Once the leader reads through the first verse, the audience will catch on and will join in the rest of the verses.

Over in the meadow,
　　In the sand, in the sun,
Lived an old mother toad
　　And her little toadie one.
"Wink!" said the mother;
　　"I wink," said the one:
So he winked and he blinked
　　In the sand, in the sun.

Over in the meadow,
　　Where the streams run blue,
Lived an old mother fish
　　And her little fishes two.
"Swim!' said the mother;
　　"We swim," said the two:
So they swam and they leaped
　　Where the stream runs blue.

27

Over in the meadow,
In a hole in a tree,
Lived a mother bluebird
And her birdies three.
"Sing!" said the mother;
"We sing," said the three:
So they sang and were glad
In the hole in the tree.

MR. NOBODY

Let the children supply the refrain.

I know a funny little man,
As quiet as a mouse,
Who does the mischief that is done
In everybody's house!
There's no one ever sees his face,
And yet we all agree
That every plate we broke was cracked
By Mr. Nobody.

'Tis he who always tears our books,
Who leaves the door ajar,

He pulls the buttons from our shirts,
  And scatters pins afar;
That squeaking door will always squeak,
  For, prithee, don't you see,
We leave the oiling to be done
  By Mr. Nobody.

The finger marks upon the door
  By none of us are made,
We never leave the blinds unclosed,
  To let the curtains fade.
The ink we never spill; the boots
  That lying round you see
Are not our boots—they all belong
  To Mr. Nobody!

29

A FARMER WENT TROTTING

Leader: A farmer went trotting
             Upon his gray mare;
Audience: Bumpety, bumpety, bump!

Leader: With his daughter behind him,
             So rosy and fair;
Audience: Lumpety, lumpety, lump!

Leader: A raven cried *"Croak"*;
             And they all tumbled down;
Audience: Bumpety, bumpety, bump!

Leader: The mare broke her knees,
               And the farmer his crown;
Audience: Lumpety, lumpety, lump!

Leader: The mischievous raven
               Flew laughing away;
Audience: Bumpety, bumpety, bump!

Leader: And vowed he would serve them
               The same the next day.
Audience: Bumpety, bumpety, bump!

POOR BILL

As the leader begins to read this, the repetition will be obvious, and the audience will chime in. The tone must show more and more anguish as the "washing" proceeds.

"Dirty again! Oh, Bill; Oh, Bill!
Come here, let me wash you!"
    That was his Mom.

"Dirty again! Oh Bill; Oh Bill!
Come here let me wash you."
    That was his Gram.

32

"Dirty again! Oh, Bill; Oh, Bill!
Come here, let me wash you."
        That was Aunt Lil.

So they washed him,
And washed him,
And washed
U N T I L
One day
There wasn't any Bill.
They had washed him
Away.

—*Marie Hall Ets*

THE WIND AND THE MOON

The listeners should blow softly at first and then harder as the wind gets angrier and the leader's voice gets louder.

Said the Wind to the Moon, "I will blow you out;
  You stare
  In the air
  Like a ghost in a chair,
 Always looking what I am about;
I hate to be watched; I will blow you out."

The Wind blew hard, and out went the Moon.
    So, deep
    On a heap
   Of clouds to sleep,
Down lay the Wind, and slumbered soon—
Muttering low, "I've done for that Moon."

He turned in his bed; she was there again!
    On high
    In the sky,
   With her one ghost eye,
The moon shone white and alive and plain.
Said the Wind—"I will blow you out again."

The Wind blew hard, and the Moon grew dim.
    "With my sledge
    And my wedge
   I have knocked off her edge!
If only I blow right fierce and grim,
The creature will soon be dimmer than dim."

He blew and he blew, and she thinned to a thread.
    "One puff
    More's enough
   To blow her to snuff!
One good puff more where the last was bred,
And glimmer, glimmer, glum will go that thread!"

He blew a great blast and the thread was gone.
    In the air
    Nowhere
   Was a moonbeam bare;
Far-off and harmless the shy stars shone;
Sure and certain the Moon was gone!

The Wind he took to his revels once more;
    On down,
    In town,
   Like a merry-mad clown,
He leaped and he halloed with whistle and roar—
"What's that?" The glimmering thread once more!

He flew in a rage—he danced and blew;
    But in vain
    Was the pain
   Of his bursting brain;
For still the broader the Moon-scrap grew
The broader he swelled his big cheeks and blew.

Slowly she grew—till she filled the night,
    And shone
    On her throne,
   In the sky alone,
A matchless, wonderful, silvery light,
Radiant and lovely, the Queen of the night.

Said the Wind, "What a marvel of power am I!
    With my breath,
    Good faith,
  I blew her to death—
First blew her right out of the sky—
Then blew her in; what a strength am I!"

But the Moon she knew nothing about the affair;
    For high
    In the sky
  With her one white eye
Motionless, miles above the air,
She had never heard the great Wind blare.

                  —*George MacDonald*

THE CHICKENS

The leader should omit the last word of each verse and let the listeners supply the rhyme.

Said the first little chicken,
    With a queer little squirm,
"I wish I could find
    A fat little —— (worm)."

Said the next little chicken,
    With an odd little shrug,
"I wish I could find
    A fat little —— (slug)."

Said the third little chicken,
    With a sharp little squeal,
"I wish I could find
    Some nice yellow —— (meal)."

Said the fourth little chicken,
    With a small sigh of grief,
"I wish I could find
    A little green —— (leaf)."

Said the fifth little chicken,
  With a faint little moan,
"I wish I could find
  A wee gravel ——— (stone)."

"Now, see here," said the mother,
  From the green garden patch,
"If you want any breakfast,
  Just come here and ——— (scratch)."

40

STORIES

Listeners will enjoy these stories even more if they participate in the actions, refrains and repetitions, together with the leader.

Don't be afraid to follow the leader; mistakes make for fun!

THE FERRYMAN

In the final game of "Sidi-Barrabah" the audience should join in and enumerate the items. The reader's voice must show a difference between Daniel and the devil: fumble and falter when reciting Daniel's part; recite the devil's part quickly and blithely so that his downfall becomes more shocking. Throughout the story, the audience will join in knocking to announce the devil's coming.

ONCE upon a time there was a man who was a ferryman. He lived with his family in a little cottage at the far end of the Island. There he had a boat with a bit of square blue sail, a stout tiller and a stern oar.

Every day, whatever the weather, he would ferry across the people from the Island to the Mainland and back again. There was no other way of crossing. It was not an easy way; the channel was full of reefs, currents and countercurrents. Above all, there was the Devil's Hole, where water would churn and swirl around and disappear in a funnel as if sucked at the bottom by a monstrous mouth. One had to know the way across and be able to navigate. Daniel knew the way across and he could navigate.

One day, as he had just sat down at the birthday of his seventh child, someone knocked at the door and asked to be ferried across. The caller was a young man going to surprise his bride on the Mainland. Could he not wait a little while, asked Daniel. There he was, Daniel, just about to celebrate the fourth birthday of his seventh child. A good meal was set on the table, which did not happen too often, and all the family was gathered together.

"The wind and the tide are against us," said Daniel. "It will take us two hours to cross. Surely your bride would understand."

But the young man would not have it any other way. And Daniel had to leave the good dinner and the party.

Well, that is life.

He pushed away from the shore, hoisted the blue square sail and gripped the tiller firmly. The young man sat facing him. The water was murky, the wind was blowing hard. Daniel set the course. They were silent.

After a while Daniel remarked briefly, "Funny! But I just cannot recall your name at all. You are not from the Island? I know everybody!"

The young man smiled and did not answer. They ran on silently, the boat tilted to one side, swishing the surface of the waves.

"But!" exclaimed Daniel suddenly, "how did you get on the Island? I did not ferry you across!"

The young man smiled and did not answer. They were in the middle of the channel. The young man got up and started toward the prow of the boat. The boat nearly capsized.

"Sit down!" shrieked Daniel. "Are you crazy? Do you want us to be caught in the Devil's Hole?"

"Why not?" said the young man turning around slowly and still smiling mysteriously. And just as he said this, Daniel's eyes fell on the rim of his trousers, and he saw the forked tip of a foot!

"Sancta Maria!" murmured Daniel, and he brought all the strength of his body to bear against the tiller. Slowly and as if reluctantly the boat veered away from the current, and in a little while, they were running peacefully toward the shore.

"A narrow escape!" said the passenger, smiling wistfully. "Yours is hard work, isn't it?"

"Yes," said Daniel, trying to avoid looking down at the forked tip of the foot. "Hard work and little pay. Most of the time we do not have much to eat at home."

"Well," said the stranger, "I guess I owe you something special since you missed one good meal because of me."

And from under his cloak he took out a heavy tinkling bag.

"Gold," he said. "Take it and be merry. Only one condition: one year from now I shall come and carry you away."

He threw the bag down, and without waiting for the boat to be made fast, he sauntered lightly onto the shore. "I will see you soon," he said cheerfully and was gone before Daniel had had time to answer.

Well. There was the gold, plenty of it, more than enough to make the whole family comfortable for years to come. And, as far as next year was concerned, it was a long way off.

So Daniel brought the gold home, and if he went on ferrying people, it was because the job was to his liking, but of worry about feeding his children he had none anymore.

And a year went by.

On the fifth birthday of his seventh child, Daniel heard a knock at the door. He opened it, and there was the devil still smiling roguishly but with a glow of greed in his eyes.

"Are you ready?" he asked.

"Yes," answered Daniel. "Only, I would like to ferry across just once more."

"Agreed," said the devil. "It's all the same to me whether I pick you up here or across. Besides, I enjoy a ride."

So they went. Daniel pushed away from the shore; he hoisted the square blue sail and gripped the tiller firmly. The devil sat facing him.

It was a beautiful summer day, but the wind was strong. When they were in the middle of the channel, and the wind was blowing the hardest, Daniel, without the slightest warning, shifted the sail, pushed the tiller all the way and brought the boat about so swiftly and unexpectedly that the devil lost his balance and fell into the water.

Daniel did not wait to see what happened to the devil. He gave the boat all the canvas it could stand, and away he flew, back to the Island. When he reached home the sun was setting, and the day on which the devil was to carry him away had passed.

And a year went by.

On the sixth birthday of his seventh child, Daniel heard a knock at the door. He opened it, and there was the devil. He was not smiling but he was none too angry, only there was a glow of greater greed in his eyes.

"Are you ready?" he asked.

"Yes," answered Daniel, "only I would like . . ."

"No!" cut in the devil sharply. "No more ferrying across."

"But I was not going to say that!" protested Daniel. "Oh, well, never mind."

"What was it you were going to say?" asked the devil, as curious as all devils are.

"Oh, nothing! Only that I would like to play one more game of bowling."

Now all devils love bowling. In summer it is their favorite game: they roll the balls and knock the pins. When there is a thunderstorm you hear the folks say, "Oh, oh, the devil is playing at ninepins!"

So when Daniel mentioned bowling, the devil could not resist the suggestion.

"Agreed," said he. "It is all the same to me whether I carry you away before or after a bowling game. Besides, I enjoy bowling."

So they went and they bowled and they bowled. And sometimes the devil won, and sometimes Daniel won. And the sun was going down.

"Time to go," said the devil. "Too bad! Such a nice game!"

"Yes," said Daniel, "but I wager that you cannot do it the way I can."

"What do you mean?" asked the devil.

"I can throw the ball and knock all the pins down with my right hand while my left hand is tied behind my back."

"I am sure I can do that, too," said the devil.

"I don't believe it," said Daniel. "It is easy to lose one's balance."

"To lose one's balance!" cried the devil stung to the quick. "Indeed! I will show you! Tie my left hand behind my back."

Daniel tied the devil's left hand behind his back. He tied it with a rope which went around and around the devil's body, and he made it fast in back.

The devil seized the ball with his right hand, he ran forward and rolled it down the alley and knocked all the pins down.

"There!" he said triumphantly. "Now let us see you do it!"

"No," said Daniel quietly, "I don't feel like it. You did it so well. I think I shall go home."

"Home!" cried the devil. "My dear man, have you forgotten that we are bound for quite another place? Quick! Untie my hand that I may carry you away."

But nonchalantly Daniel strolled away. The angry devil ran after him and tried to get hold of him. But he simply could not do it with only one hand, and finally he went away full of shame.

When Daniel reached home, the sun was setting and the day on which the devil was to carry him away had passed.

And a year went by.

On the seventh birthday of his seventh child, Daniel heard a knock at the door. He opened it, and there was the devil. He was not smiling. He looked angry and there was a glow of the greatest kind of greed in his eyes.

"Are you ready?" he asked grimly.

"Daddy! Daddy!" called the children. "Come and tell us what you bought at the fair of Sidi-Barrabah!"

"Sidi-Barrabah!" repeated the devil. "What is that?"

"Oh, a fair, just a fair," said Daniel apologetically.

"Never heard of it!" said the devil. "Strange! Tell me something about it."

"Gladly," said Daniel. "Won't you come in? Here is a gentleman, children, who wants to play with us."

"Play?" inquired the devil suspiciously. "Is it a game?"

"Yes," said Daniel.

"I don't play with you anymore," said the devil darkly.

"You do not have to play," retorted Daniel. "Watch us and you will know about it. Are you ready, children? Then let us start:

    I go to the fair of Sidi-Barrabah, and what do I buy?

    A horse."

The second child went on:

    "I go to the fair of Sidi-Barrabah and what do I buy?

    A horse

      and a sleigh."

The third child went on:

    "I go to the fair of Sidi-Barrabah and what do I buy?

    A horse

      a sleigh

        and a top."

The fourth child went on:

    "I go to the fair of Sidi-Barrabah and what do I buy?

    A horse

      a sleigh

        a top

          and a cake."

And so on until it came back to Daniel, and by that time

the list of purchases to remember was quite long. And they started another round and it was more and more difficult not to forget any word. If anyone skipped or misplaced a word, he lost one point, and after losing three points he was out of the game.

The devil was intensely interested, and as the children gradually fell out and Daniel remained the winner, he said:

"Let us play it, you and I. But as I do not want to be tricked again I shall set the rules down right now: there is no 'losing' point; each of us will stake his all and we shall play thirteen words, no more, no less."

"And if I win?" asked Daniel.

"You mean if you remember every word and in its right place?"

"Yes," said Daniel.

"In that case we both win, because there is not the slightest doubt that I shall be able to repeat every word too."

"But suppose you don't," insisted Daniel.

The devil roared with laughter.

"But it cannot be! It is impossible, unthinkable, preposterous! You will soon see why. Listen, my dear fellow, to show you how ridiculous your question is, I shall dare make a bargain with you: if I lose the game, you are free."

"Agreed," said Daniel. "Let us start:
    I go to the fair of Sidi-Barrabah and what do I buy?
        A whip."
The devil: "I go to the fair of Sidi-Barabah and what do I buy?
        A whip
            and a chimera."

Daniel: "I go to the fair of Sidi-Barrabah and what do I buy?
  A whip
    a chimera
      and an apple pie."
The devil: "I go to the fair of Sidi-Barrabah and what do I buy?
    A whip
      a chimera
        an apple pie
          and a cockatoo."
Daniel: "I go to the fair of Sidi-Barrabah and what do I buy?
    A whip
      a chimera
        an apple pie
          a cockatoo
            and a cow."
The devil: "I go to the fair of Sidi-Barrabah and what do I buy?
      A whip
        a chimera
          an apple pie
            a cockatoo
              a cow
                and a fez."
Daniel: "I go to the fair of Sidi-Barabah and what do I buy?
      A whip
        . . . . . a chimera
          an apple pie
            . . . . . a cockatoo

a cow

a . . . . f . . . f-ez

and a sail."

The devil: I go to the fair of Sidi-Barrabah and what do I buy?

A whip

a chimera

an apple pie

a cockatoo

a cow

a fez

a sail

and a hippopotamus."

Daniel: I go to the fair of Sidi-Barrabah and what do I buy?

A whip

a chimera

an apple pie

a cock . . . atoo

a cow

. . . . a fez

a sail

a hi-po-po-ta-mus

and a bee."

The devil: "I go to the fair of Sidi-Barrabah and what do I buy?

A whip

a chimera

an apple pie

a cockatoo

a cow

53

                    a fez
                 a sail
                    a hippopotamus
                 a bee
                    and a sceptre."
Daniel: "I go to the fair of Sidi-Barrabah and what do I buy?
   A whip
      a chimera
         an apple pie
            a cockatoo
         a cow
         a fez
            a sail
               a hi-po-po-ta-mus
            a bee
                  a . . . a . . . a . . . sceptre
               and a staff."
The devil: "I go to the fair of Sidi-Barrabah and what do I
buy?
      A whip
         a chimera
            an apple pie
               a cockatoo
            a cow
            a fez
               a sail
                  a hippopotamus
               a bee
                  a sceptre

                    54

a staff

and a tiara."

Daniel: "I go to the fair of Sidi-Barrabah and what do I buy?

A whip

a chimera

an apple pie

a cockatoo

a cow

. . . . a fez

a sail

. . . . a hi-po-po-ta-mus

. . . . a bee

. . . . a sceptre

. . . . a staff

. . . . a tiara

. . . .

. . . .

and. . .and. . .and. . ."

"And what?" shouted the devil, dancing wildly with joy, all ready to seize his prey. "And what?"

"And a cross," said Daniel. Then he turned to face the devil.

But there was no one there. Daniel had said the one word that the devil could not repeat.

The devil had gone and he never came back.

— *Claire Bishop*

55

THE LEOPARD'S DAUGHTER

Each time an animal "dances the dance of war," everyone raises both arms high and shakes clenched fists to show anger. When animals "dance the dance of peace," lay both palms together and bow your head in peace. The leader must be sure to call the count on each spear-throwing episode dramatically, varying the tone and speed of the count. Fling up your arm to show the thrust of the spear and clap your hands dramatically when the spear is finally caught.

ONCE upon a time, in Liberia, there lived a leopard who had a very beautiful daughter. This daughter grew up and news of her beauty spread near and far.

All the beasts of the forest hearing of her arose and came to ask for the hand of this daughter in marriage.

The leopard found himself in the greatest of embarrassment. He was a friend to all of them and for this reason did not wish to offend anyone by refusal.

But a new thought came to the leopard. He prepared a great feast and invited all who sought to marry his daughter. They assembled one by one. When the feast had reached its climax, he took his spear and threw it high, and said, "He who wants this my daughter to be his wife, that one must take this spear, hurl it into the air, and count to ten before catching it. To him

who counts to ten before catching it, I will give my daughter. Each one may have a turn, but before throwing the spear he must dance the dance of war to show he is willing to fight for his wife; then, he must dance the dance of peace to show that there is no anger in his heart toward anyone."

All the animals were glad to hear these words. They all thought there was nothing so easy as that. Sir Elephant rose in all his majesty and claimed that since he was King of the forest, he would, therefore, be the first to attempt throwing the spear. The truth was, he feared that, the task being so easy, some other might succeed before his turn was over.

"Yes, indeed," agreed the leopard. "Sir Elephant must have the first turn. It is only fitting and proper for the King of the Animals to be first."

Then the elephant danced the dance of war to show that he was willing to fight for what he wanted; next, he danced the dance of peace to prove there was no anger in his heart, and then, with all his might, he threw the spear high and began counting. "One, two, three," but before he could say "four," the spear fell down.

So, of course, he could not be given the leopard's daughter in marriage.

The buffalo then arose and came forth, saying, "I am the Vice-king of the forest and next to King Elephant. Therefore, I will be the next to throw the spear." Upon saying this, he proceeded to dance the dance of war to show he was willing to fight for a wife; next, he danced the dance of peace to show there was no anger in his heart toward anyone. Then he took the spear, threw it high, and began to count, "One, two, three, four, five, six, seven, eight," but before he could say "nine" down fell the spear.

So he, too, could not get Leopard's daughter in marriage. So they all tried one by one, but none of them succeeded in counting to ten before catching the spear.

The leopard's daughter, therefore, would have been without a husband all her life, because her father had promised that only he would get her who could count to ten before catching the spear. Since none had succeeded, it would have been most unfair for the leopard to give her to someone who had not tried to count to ten.

The angry animals rose from their seats, and began to grumble as they started to leave. "It was all a trick! The leopard did not intend to select a son-in-law. He knew all along that it is impossible to catch a spear before the count of ten!"

But just at this point one little dwarf antelope came forth, protesting. "But I want my turn! I haven't had a turn . . . and the leopard said that everyone was to have a turn!"

The other animals broke out in a great laugh, and with disgust and resentment they said, "Now, Dwarf Antelope, if we great animals of the forest have tried and failed, what do you expect to do? It would be a great insult to us all for you to try. It would have been entirely different if you had tried before us, but not after us."

But the leopard spoke up. "I did indeed say that everyone must have his turn. How in the world are we to know beforehand who is able to throw the spear and count to ten before catching it unless we allow everyone to try? Therefore, the dwarf antelope shall have a trial."

The dwarf antelope then stood up. He danced the dance of war to show that he would fight for what he wanted; next, he danced the dance of peace to prove that there was no anger in his heart. Then, he took the spear which seemed taller than himself and threw it high into the air with all his might. "Five and five are ten," he shouted and caught the spear as it came down.

The dwarf antelope had caught the spear and was the winner of the leopard's daughter. Mind you, the leopard did not say *how* you were to count to ten, and there are more ways to count to ten than by saying, "One, two, three," and so on.

Thus, we learn that we must not judge a person's abilities by his looks without giving him a chance to show all he can do. And there is more than one way to do a job!

— Liberian Folk Tale
Retold by Harold Courlander

THE KING WITH
THE TERRIBLE TEMPER

The leader divides the group into five units as indicated. Each group responds with appropriate response when its cue is given in the telling of the story.

	CUE	RESPONSE
Group 1	The King	*G-r-r-r*
Group 2	Fat Daughter	*Ka-plunk*
Group 3	Thin Daughter	*Whistle*
Group 4	Beautiful Daughter	*A-a-ahh*
Group 5	Handsome Prince	*A-ha*
All	Galloping Horse	*All make galloping sounds with feet*

THERE was once a king with a terrible temper (*G-r-r-r*). He had three beautiful daughters. The eldest was very fat (*Ka-plunk*); the second was exceedingly thin (*Whistle*); but the youngest was very beautiful (*A-a-ahh*).

Now in a nearby country there lived a handsome prince (*A-ha*). One day he came to the palace of the king with a terrible temper (*G-r-r-r*).

"I have come," said he, "to seek a wife among your daughters" (*Ka-plunk, Whistle, A-a-ahh*). First he was presented

to the eldest and, well, the heaviest daughter (*Ka-plunk*).

"She would eat too much," said the handsome prince (*A-ha*). Then appeared the daughter who was very thin (*Whistle*). She did not please him either, and he said, "But I heard that you had a young and beautiful daughter!" (*A-a-ahh*). This displeased the king with a terrible temper (*G-r-r-r*). Said he, "You can't rob my nursery for a bride!"

"Well," came the reply, "I cannot love your oldest daughter (*Ka-plunk*), and I don't like your thin daughter (*Whistle*).

Just then on the stairway appeared the youngest and most beautiful daughter (*A-a-ahh*). Rapture filled the heart of the handsome prince (*A-ha*) and he cried, "I will take your youngest daughter!"

His words greatly angered the king with the terrible temper (*G-r-r-r*).

"Call out the guards," he thundered, "and turn out this upstart of a prince" (*A-ha*).

But the suitor immediately seized the willing princess (*A-a-ahh*) in his arms and rushed out. When the royal court reached the door, all they could see was a cloud of dust raised by the hoofs of the galloping horse (*galloping sounds which gradually die away*).

So ends the romantic tale of the king with a terrible temper (*G-r-r-r*), his fat daughter (*Ka-plunk*), his thin daughter (*Whistle*), the youngest and the most beautiful daughter (*A-a-ahh*), and the handsome prince (*A-ha*), with the galloping horse (*galloping sounds with feet*).

THE GIRL WHO USED HER WITS

The audience should join the leader in bowing low to Honorable Mother-in-Law with exaggerated motions. The leader must "boo-hoo" and weep with abandon. For an added element of surprise, when the plot so dictates at the end, the leader may suddenly hold up a Chinese lantern and then a Chinese fan, both of which have been hidden beforehand.

THERE lived once a long time ago in China, a woman named Fow Chow who had two sons. These sons married young girls from a village some distance away, and when the wedding festivities were over, they brought their wives home to live with their mother.

Now Lotus-Blossom and Moon-Flower, the two daughters-in-law, were, although somewhat stupid, good and obedient young women. They were always very respectful to their mother-in-law. They waited upon her, made her tea whenever she wished it, and served her her bowl of rice and stewed meat, or salt fish and vegetables, three times a day on her little carved red lacquer table in the best blue china dishes. But, though they were always thus obedient to the head of the family, they were forever coming to the place where she sat in state in the house, bowing low before her and begging respectfully, "Honorable Mother-in-Law, we pray you, give us your permission to go for a few days and pay a visit in the village where we were born. We are so homesick."

Fow Chow grew wearied at last with their always wanting to leave home to go visiting, so she thought to herself, "I will find a way to end this once and for all."

The next time the two young brides came, bowed low before her, and made their request, she said, "Yes, my little pheasants, you may certainly go and pay a visit in your old village. Go as soon as you like. But remember this—you must bring me back when you come, the only two things I desire in all the world, or you shall never again return to your husbands and your home!"

"Oh, thank you Honorable Mother-in-Law, we will gladly bring you whatever you like," cried the two thoughtless young women.

"Very well then," said Fow Chow. "You, Lotus-Blossom, shall bring me back some fire, wrapped in paper, and you, Moon-Flower, shall bring me wind wrapped in paper."

So anxious were the young girls to be off, that they promised at once to bring back what the honored lady asked, without stopping to think how they should ever be able to get such remarkable presents.

They took leave of their husbands and started at once, chatting gaily together on the way. Through the crowds of pigs, and fowls and children in the village street they tripped, past rows of little, one-story houses with quaintly carved, gay colored porches, and out the gate of the village. They made their way well along the road and put many a field of indigo, rice and sugar cane behind them, when suddenly it came over

Lotus-Blossom just what her mother-in-law had asked of her. She must bring back some fire wrapped in paper or she could never again return to her husband or her home. Fire wrapped in paper—BUT THAT WAS NOT POSSIBLE!

On the instant, Lotus-Blossom stopped short in the road and began to cry. And when Lotus-Blossom began to cry, Moon-Flower stopped too and remembered what she had been ordered to bring back—wind wrapped in paper! Who could ever do such a thing?

So Lotus-Blossom and Moon-Flower both flung themselves down by the roadside and cried together. "Never, never, never," they sobbed, "can we go home again."

As they sat there feeling miserable, along toward them from the fields came a young girl riding on a water-buffalo. She stopped before them and asked, "Why are you crying?"

The only answer was "Boo-hoo! Boo-hoo! Boo-hoo!"

"Crying will not help matters," said the girl. "It is silly to cry. It is much better to consider and see if you cannot find a way out of your difficulties. Tell me what troubles you."

So at last the two young women dried their tears long enough to tell her of their trouble.

"Well," said the girl, "it is true you have been thoughtless and heedless, but if you are ready now to use your wits, we may still find a way out of the matter. Come home with me; we will put our heads together and see if we cannot think of a way for you to fulfill your mother-in-law's commands."

Now Lotus-Blossom and Moon-Flower had never even dreamed of thinking, but seeing that the girl honestly hoped to help them, they got up behind her on the water-buffalo and

went off with her. When they reached her father's house, they all sat down on the floor of the porch and began to consider.

"Fire wrapped in paper, fire wrapped in paper," repeated the girl. Suddenly the girl sprang to her feet. "But of course," she said, "fire wrapped in paper!" And she ran into the house. In a few moments she returned and in her hand she held, lo! a paper lantern as round as the moon, and inside the lantern was a lighted candle!

"Ah," cried Lotus-Blossom, raising her hands joyously toward the lantern, "There you have it! The very thing for me to take back to my honorable mother-in-law—fire wrapped in paper."

But Moon-Flower was still frowning; she had thought of no way whereby she could fulfill her mother-in-law's command.

So their hostess sat down between them again and thought for a time longer. "Wind wrapped in paper, wind wrapped in paper," she mumbled. "But of course, wind wrapped in paper," she said again, and rose once more, went into the house and returned with a beautifully painted fan.

"Take this and wave it back and forth!" she cried to Moon-Flower. The young wife did as she was told, and behold! the paper carried wind against her face!

"Wind wrapped in paper!" cried Moon-Flower in astonishment. "Oh, thank you, thank you. Now I too may return home to my husband."

So the two young women gratefully took leave of the girl who used her wits. They forgot all about paying a visit to their native village, but set out immediately for the home of their husbands.

Fow Chow saw them coming and was greatly surprised. She did not even wait for them to come to her, as she did on most occasions, but went to meet them at the doorway.

"Have there come to this family daughters-in-law who do not obey their mother-in-law?" she cried sternly. "Have you come here without fire wrapped in paper and wind wrapped in paper?"

As she spoke, Lotus-Blossom held up her paper lantern with fire inside it, and Moon-Flower began to send the wind against her mother-in-law's face by gently waving her paper fan.

"Well, someone has done some thinking!" the honored lady cried. "Come into the house and serve me with tea!" As they all sipped their tea from the blue china dishes on the red lacquer table, the lantern swung gaily above their heads and they cooled themselves with the paper fan. As for Fow Chow—that honorable lady smiled to herself contentedly, for she had missed her two young daughters-in-law and was glad that they had returned.

—Chinese Folk Tale

THE SEARCH:
WHO GETS THE CHIEF'S DAUGHTER?

This is a story without an end; each listener must make his own ending. The leader can ask for individual opinions on who should have won the bride and how the story should be ended.

THERE were three brothers who wanted to marry the same girl. She was the daughter of a powerful Chief. Each of the brothers made it known that he wished to have her.

The Chief called them to his house and said: "In the forest live the Mmoatia, the Little People. My daughter wants one of them to be her servant. Whichever of you first brings her one of the Little People, this man shall be her husband."

The three brothers went away and talked about what the Chief had said. One of them asked, "Wherever will we find the Mmoatia? Many people speak of them, but few people see them."

Another brother said, "Yes, who knows where they are to be found?"

And the third said, "Where their village is is not known to us, but it is somewhere in the great forest. Let us look for them."

Each of the brothers had special magic. The first had a

magical mirror. If he looked into his mirror, he could see things that were happening anywhere in the world. The second brother had a magic hammock, which would take him anywhere he wanted to go. The third brother had the power to bring the dead back to life.

They set out together to find the place where the Mmoatia lived. They traveled many days in the great forest. Whenever they met someone on the trail, they asked, "Do you know where the Mmoatia are to be found?" But no one could help them.

One day the first brother looked into his magic mirror, and he saw that the Chief's daughter had died. He told what he had seen. They said to each other, "Why should we search any longer for the Mmoatia? Now it is useless." They discussed it.

The third brother said, "I have the power to bring the dead back to life. If we could only return quickly, I could save her."

The second brother said, "I have the power to take us home. Enter my hammock."

The three brothers got into the hammock. It carried them back to their village instantly. They went to the Chief's house, and the third brother used his magic power and brought the Chief's daughter back to life.

Then the Chief declared:

"You searched in the forest; you did not find the Mmoatia. Yet you returned, and my daughter who had died, you brought back to life. You are three, and all of you had a hand in it. But I have only one daughter. Only one of you can be my son-in-law. To the one who did the most, to him will I give my daughter."

One brother had seen in his mirror that the girl had died.

One had transported them back from the forest in his hammock.

One had revived the girl from death.

Which one deserved the reward?

EBENEZER-NEVER-COULD-SNEEZER

An audience-participation story. Everyone sneezes dramatically as the story proceeds, until, at the end, the whole group has accelerated its sneezing in rhythm to sound like a rushing railroad train!

EBENEZER-NEVER-COULD-SNEEZER was a wonderful old French soldier. Years long ago he had been retired from Napoleon's army with a pension of one cheese a week for as long as he lived. He could do ANYTHING. He could tell stories by the hour. He never seemed to begin a story. He never seemed to end a story. But he could tell them all the same. All the children loved to listen. He told them stories of little boys and girls he had seen when he had been a soldier in Napoleon's armies; little boys and girls in Italy; little boys and girls in Austria; little boys and girls in Egypt; little boys and girls in Russia.

But in spite of the fact that Ebenezer could do ANYTHING, and tell stories by the hour, there was one thing he could not do. He simply could not sneeze. You might suppose it was because he never caught cold. But no, it wasn't that. He sometimes did catch cold. You might suppose it was because he never shook pepper in his soup. But no, it wasn't that. He sometimes did shake pepper in his soup. The reason he couldn't

75

sneeze was because he had no nose to sneeze with. What? No nose? Oh dear, how did that happen?

Ebenezer had a nose when he was a baby. He had a nose when he was a small boy. He had a nose when he was a young man. He had a nose when he marched away with Napoleon's army to fight for France. He had a nose before the battle of Austerlitz. But after the battle of Austerlitz his nose was gone. A cannonball tweaked it off and took it away. And that's why he never could sneeze. It wasn't because he never caught cold. It wasn't because he never shook pepper in his soup. It was because he had no nose to sneeze with.

Now the strange part was that sometimes Ebenezer wanted to sneeze very badly. Though his nose had been tweaked off by a cannonball, still, sometimes, he could feel his nose itching. And, oh, how he wanted to sneeze. He could throw back his head, open his mouth, close his eyes, and say, "Ah-ah-ah," or he could say, "Ker-ker-ker-," just as well as you or anyone else. But he could not say a single, "Choo!" Just imagine getting ready to say a good, satisfying "Choo!" and then not being able to say it. It was dreadful.

One morning Ebenezer had what he thought was a very brilliant idea. He would make himself a wooden nose. In the woodpile he found just the piece of wood he needed. With his pocketknife he whittled out a nose of wood that looked very much like the nose he had before the battle of Austerlitz. It was a very large nose, but that suited Ebenezer's purpose so much the better. In the end of where the nostrils would naturally be, he bored a hole as large as the mouth of a bottle. Into his hole he fitted a corkstopper just as you would in a bottle.

He fastened his wooden nose in place with glue, put a cork-screw in one of his pockets and sat down in the sun to wait until he should feel like sneezing.

Presently, sure enough, Ebenezer felt a sneeze coming and trembled all over with excitement. Soon he would know whether his new wooden nose was a success or a failure. Hope-fully he threw back his head, opened his mouth, closed his eyes and said, "Ah-ah-ah-!" Oh dear, oh dear, where had he put that corkscrew. Fast as he could, he screwed it into the cork-stopper in the end of his nose, and just at the end of another, "Ah-ah-ah-," he gave it a quick pull and out it came with a loud, "Pop!"

He tried it again. "Ah-ah-ah-POP!" "Ker-ker-ker-POP!" Well, that was something. But after all, it was a disappoint-ment. He couldn't really feel satisfied with an "Ah-ah-ah-POP!" or a "Ker-ker-ker-POP!" when what he wanted with all his heart was a good loud, "Ah-ah-ah-CHOO!" or a "Ker-ker-ker-CHOO!" "I am afraid," he said to himself in despair, "that I shall never, never sneeze again!" So he threw away the corkscrew. He threw away the corkstopper. And he threw away the wooden nose.

But even at that moment of his greatest disappointment, affairs were shaping in the world outside his village that were going to bring Ebenezer a very happy surprise. There came a rumor that the new railroad from Paris to the sea would run right smack through the village. With a yawn and a stretch the sleepy little town woke up and began to buzz with talk. "A railroad! What do you think of that!" said everybody to every-body else. "We'll have a station, too," they said, "where trains will arrive and depart just as they do in Paris." So it went. Buzz, buzz, buzz; how their tongues ran on. The more they talked of the railroad, the more excited they became. The Town Fathers renamed the streets for famous boulevards of Paris. The Mayor began to carry a cane and wear a silk hat. The Jack-of-all-trades mended the clock in the town hall steeple, and for the first time in half a century people could tell what time it was once more.

For months the rumors flew. For months the rumors were confirmed. For months they worked on plans. For months they worked on the tracks. For months on the station. Until finally, the day of the first train arrived. No one in the village had ever seen a railroad train, or a railroad engine, so they made a gala day of it and flocked to the station. And of course Ebenezer was there, too.

The new station shone like a dandelion in its fresh coat of yellow paint. The new tracks disappeared in one direction toward Paris and in the other direction toward the sea. The people were so excited that half of them were talking and half of them were laughing. Then the half that had been laughing began to talk, and the half that had been talking began to laugh, until they were so mixed up that everyone was talking out of one side of his mouth and laughing out of the other side of his mouth at the same time. You never heard such a bedlam! In the midst of it the town hall clock struck eleven. The train was due.

"H-oooooooooooo-h-ooooooooooooo-hoo-hoo!" Right on the dot the train whistled. Right on the dot it appeared in sight. Right on the dot it drew up at the station, bell ringing, steam escaping, engine panting, brakes grinding. Everybody shouted. Babies screamed and dogs barked. People waved from everywhere on the station platform. Ebenezer waved both hands at once. "Rat-tat-tat" down the steps of the car came the Conductor's heels with the Conductor after them, throwing out his swelling chest as he came. He bowed. He beamed. He strutted. He shook hands with the Station Agent. He shook hands with the Mayor. He shook hands with the Mayor's new cane. He shook hands with everybody, including Ebenezer, until it was time for the train to depart.

Oh, that was a big moment for Ebenezer! Just as the Conductor shouted "A-lllll aboard!", just as the engine bell began to ring, just as the Engineer put his hand on the throttle, Ebenezer felt a sneeze coming. Back flew his head. Open flew his mouth. Tight shut his eyes. "Ah-ah-ah," said Ebenezer. "CHOO!" said the engine. Oh it was a great big whacker of a choo, a delicious choo, the noisiest, juiciest CHOO you ever heard. "Ah-ah-ah-CHOO!" "Ker-ker-ker-CHOO!" The first good, satisfying sneeze Ebenezer had had since before the battle of Austerlitz! He kept it up as long as the train was in sight.

From that day on, Ebeenzer saved all his sneezes for train time. He knew when every train would depart and never missed a train. He would wait until the Conductor called, "A-lllll aboard!" He would wait until the engine bell rang and the Engineer put his hand on the throttle. Then he would throw back his head, open his mouth, shut his eyes and say, "Ah-ah-ah-" and "CHOO" would say the engine. Ah-ah-ah-choo-choo! Ker-ker-ker-choo-choo! Ah-ah-ah-ker-choo-choo-choo! Ah-ker-choo-choo-choo! Ah-ker-choo-choo! Ah-ker-choo! Ah-ker-choo! Ah-ker-choo! Ahker-choo, akherchoo, ahkerchoo-ahker-choo-ahkerchoo-ahkerchoo!

There now if you have your breath again after all that sneezing, here's the end of it. To this very day when the little boys and girls in that village hear the trains leaving the station, they laugh and say, "There goes Ebenezer-Never-Could-Sneezer's nose."

—*Gilbert S. Pattillo*

THE LADY'S ROOM

Each time the fairy kicks at the wall, the reader should hold both palms out straight and in a chopping, quick, up-and-down motion, move each palm up and down alternately, saying rapidly, "Kick, kick, kick, kick, etc." The listeners will soon follow suit.

A Lady once lived in a room that was as white as snow. Everything in it was white; it had white walls and ceiling, white silk curtains, a soft white sheepskin carpet, and a little ivory bed with a white linen coverlet. The Lady thought it was the most beautiful room in the world, and lived in it as happy as the day was long.

But one day she looked out of her window and saw the beautiful green grass shining like a carpet on the ground and all at once she began to sigh.

"Oh, dear!" sighed the Lady.

"What's the matter with *you*, Lady?" said a tiny voice at the window, and there, sitting on the sill, was a Fairy no bigger than your finger, and on her feet she wore two little shoes as green as grass in April.

"Oh, Fairy!" cried the Lady. "I am so tired of this plain white room! I would be so happy if only it were a green room!"

"*Right* you are, Lady!" said the Fairy, and she sprang on to the bed, and lay on her back, and kicked away at the wall with her two little feet. In the twinkling of an eye the white room turned into a green one, with green walls and ceiling, green net curtains, a carpet like moss in the woods, and a little green bed with a green linen coverlet.

"Oh, thank you, Fairy!" cried the Lady, laughing for joy. "Now I *shall* be as happy as the day is long!"

The Fairy flew away, and the Lady walked about her green room gay as a bird. But one day she looked out of the window and smelled the flowers growing in the garden and all at once she began to sigh.

"Oh, dear!" sighed the Lady. "Oh, dear!"

"What's the matter with *you*, Lady?" asked a tiny voice, and there on the windowsill sat the Fairy, swinging her two little feet in shoes as pink as rose-petals in June.

"Oh, Fairy!" cried the Lady, "I made such a mistake when I asked you for a green room. I'm so tired of my green room! What I really meant to ask for was a pink room!"

"*Right* you are, Lady!" said the Fairy, and jumped on the bed, and lay on her back, and kicked at the wall with her two little feet. All in a moment the green room changed into a pink one, with pink walls and ceiling, pink damask curtains, a carpet like rose-petals, and a little rosewood bed with a pink linen coverlet.

"Oh, thank you, Fairy!" cried the Lady, clapping her hands. "This is just the room I have always wanted!"

The Fairy flew away, and the Lady settled down in her pink room, as happy as a rose.

But one day she looked out of her window and saw the leaves dancing in the garden, and before she knew it she was sighing like the wind.

"Oh, dear!" sighed the Lady. "Oh, dear, oh, dear!"

"What's the matter with *you*, Lady?" cried the Fairy's tiny voice, and there was the Fairy hopping on the windowsill in a pair of shoes as golden as lime leaves in October.

"Oh, Fairy!' cried the Lady. "I am so tired of my pink room! I can't think how I ever came to ask you for a pink room, when all the time a golden room was what I really wanted."

"*Right* you are, Lady!" said the Fairy, and she leaped on to the bed, lay on her back, and kicked at the wall with her two little feet. Quicker than you can wink, the pink room turned golden, with walls and ceiling like sunshine, and curtains like golden cobwebs, and a carpet like fresh-fallen lime leaves, and a little gold bed with a gold cloth coverlet.

"Oh, thank you, thank you!" cried the Lady, dancing for joy. "At last I really have the very room I wanted!" The Fairy flew away, and the Lady ran around her golden room as light-hearted as a leaf. But one night she looked out of the window and saw the stars shining on the garden and fell a-sighing, as though she would never stop.

"*Now* what's the matter with you, Lady?" said the tiny voice from the windowsill. And there stood the Fairy in a pair of shoes as black as night.

"Oh, Fairy!" cried the Lady, "it is all this golden room! I cannot *bear* my bright golden room, and if only I can have a black room instead, I will never want any other as long as I live!"

"The matter with *you*, Lady," said the Fairy, "is that you don't know *what* you want!" And she jumped on the bed, and lay on her back, and kicked away with her two little feet. And the walls fell through, and the ceiling fell up, and the floor fell down, and the Lady was left standing in the black starry night without any room at all.

—Eleanor Farjeon

WITH A WIG, WITH A WAG

Be sure to say, "Have you seen a lad," in unison each time. Say it faster and louder each successive time.

ONCE there were three brothers who had not so much as a penny between them. When the daffodils began to dance, the eldest brother said, "I'm off to try my fortune."

And away he went. He traveled about for a long time until he saw a little white house. Walking up boldly, he knocked on the door. An old hag with two beady eyes and a tight pursed mouth cracked it open.

"May I stay the night?" asked the eldest brother, for the shadows were getting long.

"Yes," allowed the hag. "Come in."

And she showed him the ladder to her loft. Climbing up, he found a straw mat near the chimney and fell asleep. Toward the middle of the night a clinking noise awoke him. He crept slowly to a knothole where a chink of light showed through. Putting his eye to the hole, he saw the old hag before a little fire counting piles of money. When she finished, she put the coins in a long leather bag and hung it on a hook in her cupboard. Then she fell asleep on the warm hearthstone.

When the eldest brother heard her snoring, he climbed carefully down the ladder, opened the cupboard, shouldered the leather bag and was off out the door. He never stopped running till he came to an old meetinghouse.

The meetinghouse asked, "Will you sweep me, lad?"

"No," answered the eldest brother. "I've no time to stop." And he took to his legs again.

As the sun came up, he passed by a field.

"Boy, will you weed me?" asked the field.

"Certainly not," said the eldest brother, and he was off again, but not so briskly, for it seemed as though the bag had doubled in weight.

Soon he came to a well. As he stopped for a drink, the well asked, "Will you clean me, boy?"

"No," answered the brother without a second thought. "I've no time for that." On he went, the coins clinking at his side.

At noon he came to the meadows with a maple tree. In the maple's shade he sat down to rest.

Now when the old hag woke and found that both her treasure and the boy in the loft had disappeared, she put two and two together and reached for her birch rod. Then she was off down the road like a gust of March wind.

Going by the meetinghouse, she stopped to ask:

> *Have you seen a lad*
> *With a wig, with a wag,*
> *With a long leather bag,*
> *Who stole all the money*
> *Ever I had?*

The meetinghouse replied, "With a wig, with a wag, he came by here on his way to a field."

The old hag went on and came to the field.

> *Have you seen a lad*
> *With a wig, with a wag,*
> *With a long leather bag,*
> *Who stole all the money*
> *Ever I had?*

"With a wig, with a wag, he came by here on his way to a well," replied the field.

The old hag scurried on again and came to the well.

> *Have you seen a lad*
> *With a wig, with a wag,*
> *With a long leather bag,*
> *Who stole all the money*
> *Ever I had?*

"With a wig, with a wag, he's in yonder meadow under the maple tree," said the well.

On she went and came to the meadow. There was the eldest brother asleep under the tree. With a blow of the birch rod she did for the boy, then picked up the bag and started for home.

After some time the second brother said, "I'm off to seek my fortune." And away he went before even the sun was up. He traveled until he too came to the old hag's house and knocked on the door.

"May I stay the night?" asked the second brother.

"Yes," allowed the crone. "Come in." And she showed him the ladder to the loft. He found the mat by the chimney and quickly fell asleep. Waking in the middle of the night, he crept to the knothole and saw the old hag playing with her coins.

When the second brother heard her snoring, he climbed carefully down, found the leather bag and was off out the door.

"Will you sweep me, lad?" asked the meetinghouse as he hurried by.

"No," answered the second brother.

"Will you weed me, lad?" asked the field.

"No time to stop," said the boy.

"Will you clean me, lad?" asked the well.

"No time for that," repeated the second brother, the coins clinking at his side. On he ran until, like his eldest brother, he, too, fell asleep under the maple.

When the old crone found her bag and lodger gone for the second time, she whirled down the road like an angry wasp. The meetinghouse and the field and the well told her where the second brother had gone. Finding him, like the first, asleep under the tree, she finished off the second brother with her birch rod, picked up her bag and started for home.

Now when the youngest brother grew tired of living by himself, he too decided to seek his fortune. So one morning when the sun smiled over the hill, he started on his way. He traveled about for a long time and finally came to the house of the old hag.

Yes, he might stay the night, and she showed him the ladder

to the loft. Quickly he fell asleep, and when the clinking coins woke him, he crept to the knothole and saw the old crone stacking her money. After she went to sleep, he too found the bag and was off out the door. One foot before the other, he came to the meetinghouse.

"Will you sweep me, lad?"

Now the youngest brother always had been one to help his neighbors, so he answered, "Yes." And though it took a long time, he left no dust in the corners.

Then he ran till he came to the field.

"Will you weed me, lad?"

"Yes," answered the third brother. And furrow by furrow he pulled the weeds.

Then he went on till he came to the well.

"Will you clean me, lad?"

And though he was afraid the old woman surely would catch up with him, he cleaned with care.

At noon he came to the maple tree and sat down to get his breath.

When the old hag awoke and found both treasure and lodger gone for a third time, she was off down the road like a streak of summer lightning.

Going by the meetinghouse, she asked:

> *Have you seen a lad*
> *With a wig, with a wag,*
> *With a long leather bag,*
> *Who stole all the money*
> *Ever I had?*

The meetinghouse made no answer. In a sudden whirl of wind, shingles from its roof blew every which way, and hitting the old hag, almost killed her.

She hurried on to the field.

> *Have you seen a lad*
> *With a wig, with a wag,*
> *With a long leather bag,*
> *Who stole all the money*
> *Ever I had?*

The field replied with a cloud of dust and stones which covered the old hag and almost blinded her.

She hastened on to the well.

> *Have you seen a lad*
> *With a wig, with a wag,*
> *With a long leather bag,*
> *Who stole all the money*
> *Ever I had?*

Then the water in the well began to rise and overflow, and reaching out its cold arms, pulled her down in its shaft.

The youngest brother went merrily home. Sharing his treasure with friends, he lived to a ripe old age.

FINGER PLAYS

Finger plays are fun to do. Try some of these well-known ones and then make up your own. The first one is a good way to quiet a restless group.

FIVE LITTLE SQUIRRELS

Five little squirrels fat,
    (Hold up left hand.)
Frisking around one day.
    (Wiggle fingers.)
Soon only four were left,
For one ran away.
    (Bend thumb down in palm of hand.)
Four little squirrels fat,
Playing in a tree.
One scampered off again.
Then there were three.
    (Cover with index finger.)
Three little squirrels fat,
Didn't know what to do.
Mother Squirrel called one,
Then there were two.
    (Cover with middle finger.)
Two little squirrels fat,
Having lots of fun.
One went and hid himself,
Then there was one.
    (Cover with ring finger.)
One little squirrel fat,
Didn't know what to do.
Couldn't play all by himself,
So he ran home, too.
    (Bend little finger over and make a closed fist.)

—Emma F. Bush

TEN LITTLE FISHES

Ten little fishes were swimming in a school.
   (*Pointing to each finger in turn.*)
This one said, "Let's swim where it is cool."
This one said, "It's a very warm day."
This one said, "Come on, let's play."
This one said, "I'm as hungry as can be."
This one said, "There's a worm for me."
This one said, "Wait, we'd better look."
This one said, "Yes, it's on a hook."
This one said, "Can't we get it anyway?"
This one said, "Perhaps we may."
This one, so very brave, grabbed a bite and swam away.

THE BRAVE LITTLE INDIAN

The brave little Indian
   (*Hold index finger at side of head like a feather in the hair.*)
Went hunting for a bear.
   (*Hold hand over eyes in "seeing" gesture.*)
He looked in the woods
   (*Make sweeping gesture with hands.*)
And everywhere.

The brave little Indian
   (*Hold index finger at side of head like a feather in hair.*)
Found a big bear.
   (*Hold hand over eyes in "seeing" gesture.*)
He ran like a rabbit.
   (*Clap hands.*)
Oh, what a scare!
   (*Place hand on heart to show "scare."*)

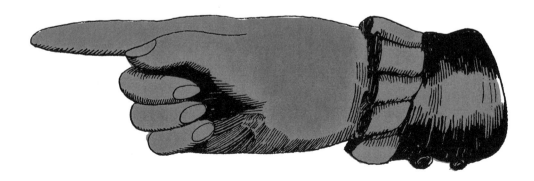

PLAYING TOGETHER

Four little boys sat on a bus,
> *(Make left hand into fist [bus]; place right hand on back of left with fingers pointing up, but bent down.)*

One named Tony and one named Gus,
> *(Hold up a finger for each child.)*

One named Woo and one named Pete,
> *(Hold up fingers; now four are up; thumb is still down.)*

Along came Hilda and wanted a seat.
> *(Pop up the thumb.)*

Five little children as different as could be.
> *(Hold up right hand.)*

Yet they are happy, like you and me.
> *(Wiggle fingers.)*

Five little children get off the bus,
> *(Walk fingers across lap.)*

Their names were Woo, Tony, Hilda, Pete and Gus.
> *(Hold up fingers one at a time in rapid order starting with the thumb.)*

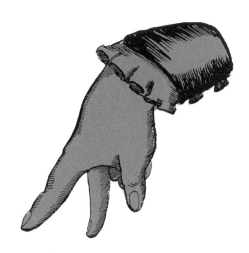

CREEPING INDIANS

The Indians are creeping,
     (Creep fingers along forearm.)
Shh . . . shh . . . shh . . . shh . . .
     (Raise fingers to lips.)
The Indians are creeping,
     (Creep fingers along forearm.)
Shh . . . shh . . . shh . . . shh . . .
     (Raise fingers to lips.)
They do not make a sound
As their feet touch the ground.
The Indians are creeping,
     (Creep fingers along forearm.)
Shh . . . shh . . . shh . . .
     (Raise fingers to lips.)

HERE'S A CUP

Here's a cup, and here's a cup,
  (Make circle with thumb and index finger
  of one hand; extend arm and repeat.)
And here's a pot of tea.
  (Make fist with one hand
  and extend thumb for spout.)
Pour a cup, and pour a cup,
  (Tip fist to pour.)
And have a drink with me.
  (Make drinking motions.)

TEN FINGERS

Follow the action as the rhyme indicates.

I have ten little fingers
And they all belong to me.
I can make them do things.
Would you like to see?
I can shut them up tight
Or open them wide.
I can put them together
Or make them all hide.
I can make them jump high,
I can make them jump low,
I can fold them quietly
And hold them just so.

RIDDLES

Riddles have been a favorite form of amusement for many centuries and throughout many countries. Number two, following, dates from 1600 and number five from 1792. Share your own favorites with your group.

1. What makes more noise than a cat caterwauling at night?

2. Two brothers we are; great burdens we bear,
    On which we are bitterly pressed;
    The truth is to say, we are full all the day,
    And empty when we go to rest.

3. Lives in winter, dies in summer,
   and grows its roots upward.

4. On what side of a tobacco
   shed does the tobacco grow
   in Connecticut?

5. Formed long ago, yet made today,
   Employed while others sleep;
   What few would like to give away
   Nor any wish to keep.

6. What's the difference between
   an orange and a monkey?

7. What grows larger the more you take from it?

8. If Mr. Jones owned a peacock and it laid an egg
in Mr. Smith's yard, who would own the egg?

9. What are the biggest ants in the world?

10. What do giraffes have that no other animal has?

11. Why did they bury President F. D. Roosevelt in New York State?

12. Four brothers have one hat. Who are they?

13. What was the name of Martha Washington's tailor's wife's niece?

14. What should you do immediately if you find an elephant in your bathtub?

SONGS

*Most of these songs can be length-
ened or shortened by adding or les-
sening the words or the actions. Be
original; change the words and actions to suit the group.*

I LOVE MY ROOSTER

Sing the first verse of the song. Give in advance the order of animals in the verses and be sure to make all the animal sounds suggested by the words.

I love my rooster, my rooster loves me,
I love my rooster by the cottonwood tree,
My little rooster goes Cocka-doodle-doo
Dee-doodle-dee-doodle-dee-doodle-dee-doo.

I love my hen, my hen loves me,
I love my hen by the cottonwood tree,
My little hen goes cluck, cluck, cluck,
My little rooster goes Cocka-doodle-doo
Dee-doodle-dee-doodle-dee-doodle-dee-doo.

I love my duck, my duck loves me,
I love my duck by the cottonwood tree,
My little duck goes quack, quack, quack,
My little hen goes cluck, cluck, cluck,
My little rooster goes Cocka-doodle-doo
Dee-doodle-dee-doodle-dee-doodle-dee-doo.

I love my sheep, etc.   (Ma-a-a-)

I love my turkey, etc.   (Gobble)

ROLL OVER

Start this song slowly so that you can go faster and faster. The last spoken line should be slow, loud and dramatic.

1. Ten in the bed, and the little one said:
   "Roll over! Roll over!"
   They all rolled over and one fell out.

2. Nine in the bed and the little one said:
   "Roll over! Roll over!"
   They all rolled over and one fell out.

3. Eight in the bed . . .

4. Seven in the bed . . .

5. Six in the bed . . .

6. Five in the bed . . .

7. Four in the bed . . .

8. Three in the bed . . .

9. Two in the bed . . .

10. One in the bed and the little one said
    (*spoken*): "Alone at last!"

Roll Over

I KNOW A LITTLE PUPPY

Sing each line a note higher in the scale; sing "bow-wows" down the scale.

I know a little puppy, he hasn't any tail,
He isn't very chubby, he's skinny as a rail.
Although he is a puppy, he'll never be a hound,
They sell him at the butcher shop for thirty cents a pound.
Bow-wow, wow-wow, wow-wow, wow-wow.
HOT DOG!

LAZY JOHN

For more fun point to the various articles of clothing mentioned and be very dramatic when repeating, "Will you marry me? How can I marry you?"

Girls (eagerly):
> Lazy John, Lazy John, will you marry me?
> Will you marry me?

Boys (reluctantly):
> How can I marry you?
> No hat to wear . . .

Together (fast):
> Off she jumped and away she ran
> Down to the market square.
> There she bought a hat
> For Lazy John to wear.

Verse 2: No shirt to wear, etc.

Verse 3: No pants to wear, etc.

Verse 4: No socks to wear, etc.

Verse 5: No shoes to wear, etc.

Verse 6:

> *Girls:*
> > Lazy John, Lazy John, will you marry me?
> > Will you marry me?
>
> *Boys:*
> > How can I marry you?
> > With a wife and ten children at home.

Girls:

La - zy John, La - zy John, will you mar - ry me? Will you mar-ry me?

Boys:

How can I mar - ry you No hat to wear _____

All:

Off she jumped and a way she ran Down to the mar-ket square. There she bought a

Coda *Boys:*

hat for la - zy John to wear with a wife and ten chil-dren at home.

FOUND A PEANUT

Tune: "O My Darling Clementine." Group performs the actions indicated by the words, exaggerating with facial expressions.

1. Found a peanut, found a peanut,
    Found a peanut last night!
    Last night I found a peanut,
    Found a peanut last night.

2. Broke it open, broke it open,
    Broke it open last night!
    Last night I broke it open,
    Broke it open last night.

3. It was rotten, it was rotten . . .

4. Ate it anyway, ate it anyway . . .

5. Got a tummyache, got a tummyache . . .

6. Called the doctor, called the doctor . . .

7. Appendicitis, appendicitis . . .

8. Operation, operation . . .

9. Died anyway, died anyway . . .

10. Went to heaven, went to heaven . . .

11. Didn't want me, didn't want me . . .

12. Went the other way, went the other way . . .

13. Wouldn't take me, wouldn't take me . . .

14. Stayed anyway, stayed anyway . . .

15. Shovelled coal, shovelled coal . . .

16. Burnt my thumb, burnt my thumb . . .

17. It was a dream, it was a dream . . .

SWEETLY SINGS THE DONKEY

(a three-part round)

Place hands on head and flap like a donkey's ears when saying "Hee-haw."

Sweetly sings the donkey, on his way to hay;
If you don't go with him, he will run away;
Hee-haw . . . Hee-haw . . . Hee-haw . . . Hee-haw.

MARCHING TO PRETORIA

Clap your hands in rhythm for the first part of the song; stamp your feet in rhythm as you sing the chorus and pretend to march. Make up your own verses as you go along.

1. I'm with you and you're with me,
   And so we are all together,
   And so we are all together,
   And so we are all together,

   Sing with me, I'll sing with you,
   And so we'll sing together,
   As we march along.

Chorus

   We are marching to Pretoria,
   Pretoria, Pretoria.
   We are marching to Pretoria
   Pretoria, hurrah!

2. We have food, the food is good,
   And so we will eat together,
   And so we will eat together,
   And so we will eat together,

   When we eat, 'twill be a treat,
   And so let us sing together,
   As we march along.

Repeat chorus.

118

Marching To Pretoria

I AM A MUSICIAN

*Get into the spirit of this song! Make the sounds of the instruments; act out
the motions; make up a great orchestra!*

I.

Leader: I am a musician; I come from Schwabenland;

Group: We all are musicians; we come from Schwabenland;

Leader: I can play the fiddle;

119

All: We all can play the fiddle;
            Plink, plink, plink, plink, plink, plink, etc.

2.

Leader: I am a musician; I come from Schwabenland;

Group: We all are musicians; we come from Schwabenland;

Leader: I can play the trumpet;

All: We all can play the trumpet;
            Ta ta, ta ta, ta ta, etc.

3.
piano . . .

4.
bass drum . . .

5.
piccolo . . . etc.

I WENT TO THE ANIMAL FAIR

Clap your hands and stamp your feet as you sing.

I went to the animal fair,
The birds and the beasts were there.
The old baboon by the light of the moon
    was combing his auburn hair.
The monkey he got drunk.
And sat on the elephant's trunk.
The elephant sneezed and fell on his knees
And that was the end of the monk, monk, monk.
And that was the end of the monk.

UNDER THE SPREADING CHESTNUT TREE

Sing the whole song through the first time with no motions. Repeat the whole song ten consecutive times, substituting one more motion for each word each time.

"under"—hands stretched out in front
"spreading"—arms outstretched over head
"chest"—strike chest
"nut"—point to head
"tree"—arms outstretched over head
"I"—point to self
"held"—arms as though embracing
"you"—point to someone
"knee"—slap knee
"happy"—smile

Under the spreading chestnut tree,
When I held you on my knee,
Oh, how happy we could be,
Under the spreading chestnut tree.

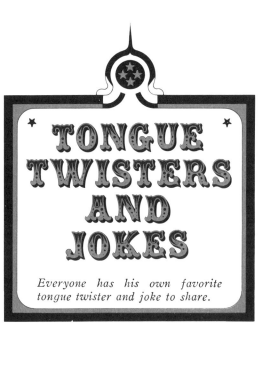

TONGUE TWISTERS AND JOKES

Everyone has his own favorite tongue twister and joke to share.

When a doctor doctors another doctor, does he doctor the doctored doctor the way the doctored doctor wants to be doctored, or does he doctor the doctored doctor the way the doctoring doctor wants to doctor the doctor?

124

Six thick thistle sticks.

Round and round the ragged robin ran.

Sheep shouldn't sleep in a shack,
Sheep should sleep in a shed.

Six snakes, slipping and sliding.

My father he left me, just as he was able,
One bowl, one bottle, one label;
Two bowls, two bottles, two labels;
Three bowls, three bottles, three labels,
and so on . . .

First boy: I'm studying to be a barber.
Second boy: Will it take long?
First boy: No, I'm learning all the short cuts.

Mary: Peanuts are fattening.
Billy: How do you know?
Mary: Did you ever see a skinny elephant?

Tommy: Aren't ants funny little things? They work and work and never play.
Johnny: Oh, I don't know about that. Every time I go on a picnic, they're there.

Mary: Has your baby sister learned to talk yet, Sally?
Sally: Oh, yes. We're teaching her to keep quiet now.

Auntie: What did Margaret get at the birthday party?
Mother: Three books, two handkerchiefs and the measles.

Pupil: This isn't fair! I don't think I deserve an absolute zero.
Teacher: Neither do I, but it's the lowest mark I can give.

Patient: Doctor, every time I drink a cup of coffee, I get a sharp pain in my eye. What should I do?
Doctor: Just take the spoon out of your cup.

COLLECTOR'S NOTE
TO STORYTELLERS
AND GROUP LEADERS

THE happy response of children and storytellers to the collection JUBA THIS AND JUBA THAT: *Story Hour Stretches for Large or Small Groups* was gratifying proof that material to fill that difficult few minutes in the middle of a formal story hour is welcome, indeed.

The stories, songs, chants, rhymes and activities in this book have been favorites of this storyteller and her listeners in public library story hours. They have provided a needed change of pace from the more formal folk tales, myths and legends that are the basis for most story hours.

An ingenious storyteller will use the selections in this collection as a steppingstone to many other materials that can be used to encourage and foster spontaneous group interaction. A well-planned story hour stretch usually ensures a successful story hour!

ACKNOWLEDGMENTS

Grateful acknowledgment is made to the following publishers and individuals, for permission to reprint copyrighted material in this book.

Addison-Wesley Publishing Company for the right to adapt the title and to reprint the text of the poem "The Fish with the Deep Sea Smile" from *Nibble, Nibble* by Margaret Wise Brown, Text © 1959 by Margaret Wise Brown. A Young Scott Book. Reprinted by permission.

The American Folklore Society for "What's This That's Got a Heart in Its Head?" from "Bermuda Folklore," by Elsie Crews Parsons in the *Journal of American Folklore,* Volume 38 (1925), p. 265. Reprinted by permission.

Boy Scouts of America for "I Know a Little Puppy" from *Cub Scout Songbook,* 1955 printing. Reprinted by permission.

Branden Press, Inc. for *The Leopard's Daughter,* Copyright © 1961 by Bruce Humphries. Reprinted by permission.

Coward, McCann & Geoghegan, Inc., and Faber and Faber, Ltd. for *The Ferryman* by Claire Bishop, Text copyright, 1941 by Coward, McCann, Inc.; copyright renewed © 1968 by Claire Bishop. Reprinted by permission.

Curtis, Brown Ltd. for "This Is the Key," "The Story of Augustus," "The Chickens," "Animal Fair," "There Was An Old Person of Dean," by Edward Lear, the first three verses of "Over in the Meadow," and "Green Grass Growing All Around" from *The Moon Is Shining Bright as Day* by Ogden Nash, published by J. B. Lippincott Company, Text copyright, 1953 by Ogden Nash. Reprinted by permission.

Doubleday and Company, Inc., for three jokes from *10,000 Jokes, Toasts, and Stories* by Lewis and Faye Copeland, Text copyright, 1939 and 1940 by Lewis and Faye Copeland. Reprinted by permission. Also to Doubleday and Company, Inc., and McClelland and Stewart, Ltd, Toronto for "I Found a Peanut," "Momma, Momma" and "Head, Shoulders, Knees and Toes" from *Sally Go Round the Sun* by Edith Fowke, Text copyright © 1970 by Edith Fowke. Reprinted by permission.

Follett Publishing Company, a division of the Follett Corporation, for "A Is for Apple" and "The Old Woman and the Pig" from *Did You Feed My Cow?* by Margaret Taylor Burroughs. Previous copyright, 1956 by Margaret Taylor. Reprinted by permission.

Grossett and Dunlap, Inc., for four jokes, three tongue twisters and three limericks from *Great Big Joke and Riddle Book* edited by Oscar Weigle, Text copyright © 1959, 1964, 1967, 1970 by Grossett and Dunlap, Inc. Also for three riddles from *A Treasury of Games* by Carl Withers, Text copyright, 1947 by Thomas Y. Crowell Company; copyright renewed © 1964 by Carl Withers. Published by Grossett and Dunlap, Inc., reprinted by permission.

Harcourt, Brace and Jovanovich, Inc. and Granada Publishing Ltd. for "The Search" from *The King's Drum* by Harold Courlander, Text copyright © 1952 by Harold Courlander. Reprinted by permission.

Holt, Rinehart and Winston, Inc. for "Mary Had a Little Lamb" and "Hickory, Dickory Dock" from *A Rocket in My Pocket* compiled by Carl Withers, Text copyright, 1948 by Carl Withers. Also for "Jeremiah" from *I Saw a Rocket Walk a Mile* by Carl Withers, Text copyright © 1965 by Carl Withers. Reprinted by permission.

Houghton, Mifflin Company for one limerick from *Anthology of Children's Literature* by Johnson, Scott and Sickels.

Informal Music Service, Delaware, Ohio, for six riddles and one tongue twister from *Fun with Folklore* © 1955. Also for "The King with a Terrible Temper" from *Handy Stunts* © 1961. Reprinted by permission.

J. B. Lippincott Company and David Higham Associates, Ltd., for "Boys' Names" and "Girls' Names" Copyright, 1933; renewed © 1961 by Eleanor Farjeon. From the book *Poems For Children* by Eleanor Farjeon, Text copyright, 1951 by Eleanor Farjeon. Reprinted by permission.

Robert B. Luce, Inc. for four fingerplays from *Let's Do Fingerplays* by Marcia Grayson, Text copyright © 1962 by Marcia Grayson. Reprinted by permission.

David McKay, Inc. for "With a Wig, with a Wag" from *With a Wig, With a Wag* by Jean Cothran, Text copyright © 1955 by Jean Cothran. Reprinted by permission.

Harold Ober Associates, Inc. and David Higham Associates, Ltd., for "The Lady's Room" from *The Little Book Room* by Eleanor Farjeon, published by Henry Z. Walck, Text copyright, 1942 by Eleanor Farjeon. Reprinted by permission.

G. Schirmer, Inc. for "Marching To Pretoria" from *Songs of the Veld* by Josef Marais, Text copyright, 1942 by G. Schirmer, Inc. Reprinted by permission.

Standard Publishing for "Playing Together" by Hazel Evans and "Five Little Squirrels" by Emma F. Bush, from *Finger Plays and How to Use Them,* Text copyright, 1952 by Standard Publishing. Reprinted by permission.

United Educators, Inc., for "Girl Who Used Her Wits" from *My Book House,* Text copyright, 1920; renewed © 1964 by The Book House for Children, Lake Bluff, Illinois. Reprinted by permission.

The Viking Press, Inc. for "Poor Bill" from *Beasts and Nonsense* by Marie Hall Ets, Text copyright, 1952 by Marie Hall Ets. Reprinted by permission.

Western Publishing Company, Inc., for "Ebenezer-Never-Could-Sneezer" by Gilbert S. Pattillo from *Story Parade,* Text copyright, 1936; copyright renewed © 1964 by Story Parade, Inc. Reprinted by permission.

World Publishing Company for "There Was an Old Man from Blackheath" and "A Silly Fellow Named Hyde" from *Humorous Poetry For Children* by William Cole, Text copyright © 1955 by World Publishing. Reprinted by permission.

The author wishes to extend many thanks to Nan Keller for "Merry Mack."

131

INDEX OF TITLES